The Rhythm of Love

25 Things that 25 Years of Marriage Taught Us

Clarence & Yalonda Lewis

ISBN: 979-8-9864418-0-1

The Rhythm of Love

Proudly self-published through Divine Legacy Publishing, www.divinelegacypublishing.com

Dedication

This book is dedicated to Symone and Nathan. For all that you are and all you will be, we love you.

- Mommy & Daddy

Acknowledgments

We thank our Lord and Savior, Jesus Christ. May he be glorified in our work. To our parents, your words of wisdom always find their mark. Thank you for all your demonstrations of love, for always supporting our stream, and for encouraging us to write this book. Mom (aka @msdurham1), we greatly appreciate your superb editing. Mom and Dad (aka @ccljr_trek and @lillie_pea) we appreciate your after-show "critiques"! And Omah (aka @linda1db) for being there when Monie needs 3 parents and a dog.

This book would not exist if it wasn't for the encouragement of our Twitch community, so many thanks to all of you. If we tried to include everyone's names, we would double the length of the book, but we are so grateful for your consistent support! Without your energy, we could not do our HeartBEATS stream every week. There have been multiple times we have struggled to go live but pushed through because of you. Thank you to everyone who encouraged us to put our truth on the page; we appreciate your belief in us!

There are a few we must mention: @docchriswright, @sumthing2say, @tsquare1969, @hrwgriffin, @klassyt, @eagle_butterfly, and @NiyaCenter thank you for your decades of friendship, support, and encouragement in real life and on-screen. Thank you to our moderators @LaDawn_225 and @Onereson who bring their stream management skills, unique gifts, and personality to The Basement. To @djeclipselive, @djirule202, @djshannellb, @djdroopy0037, and the rest of the Last Train to Friday (#LTTF) family, much love and thanks for the inspiration and true friendship. Last, but certainly not least, to @AuthorJavonda_5, our amazing writing coach and cheerleader, this book couldn't have gotten done without you!!

Tracks

Intro

In July 2021, we celebrated 25 years of marriage. It's been a rollercoaster that has taken us halfway around the world and back. We've experienced the highest highs together, like spending 6 months living in Zurich and traveling around Europe and North Africa. We've also suffered through low times, like when our eldest child was diagnosed with autism. Through it all, we leaned on one another when necessary and lifted each other up at every opportunity. We had to learn the best ways to lean and how best to lift.

During the COVID-19 lockdown of 2020, one of the things we started doing together was live-streaming on Sunday nights on Twitch (twitch.tv/djcsharp). Our stream is called HeartBEATS in The Basement and Clarence (who is a professional DJ called DJ C Sharp) plays slow jams while Yalonda chats with him and the virtual guests about music, relationships, or other fun topics. It's our time to relax from the stress of the world and connect with like-minded people online. Originally, our audience consisted of mostly family and close friends, but over time our audience grew. We developed new friendships and relationships with people from all around the world, and many people in our "Twitch community" have become like family.

For our 25th wedding anniversary, we streamed a celebratory HeartBEATS episode titled, "25 Things We've Learned in 25 Years." We thought it would be a fun way to reminisce about our quarter-century together whilst also being a way to share our milestone day with family and friends in a safe, responsible way considering the pandemic. We told stories and lessons learned, joked, laughed, disagreed, and had a great time. At the end of the night, we shut down and headed to bed like we usually would after each Sunday stream, happily recalling the highlights and discussing what we could do better next time.

Then the phone calls began.

Clarence's dad usually calls after each stream to give us his feedback, but this was different. Suddenly we had a dozen people call or text us to tell us how much they enjoyed the show. They enjoyed it not solely for its entertainment value, but more importantly, they appreciated our representation of black love. They loved our candidness about some of what it takes to achieve marital longevity. Almost everyone suggested that we should write a book.

Our first thoughts were, "Yeah right, what do we know about writing a book? What do we look like advising people on marriage? We're not counselors. We are just two people who got married out of college and have been trying to figure it out through trial and error for the past 25 years."

We brushed it off and went to bed.

The next day, much to our surprise, the phone calls and texts encouraging us to do more kept coming. So we began to reconsider. "Should we write a book? Is this something we could pull off? Could we actually write a book?" We started doing a little research and reached out to friends who are published authors to discuss the kind of commitment such an undertaking requires. They were all quite encouraging and provided us with tons of helpful information about self-publishing. After serious thought and getting over our initial trepidation, we decided to put pen to paper to try.

We modeled this book after the stream, using the "25 Things We've Learned in 25 Years" as the baseline for our chapters. When composing the original list for the stream, we each separately drafted a list of 15 lessons from our time as a married couple. Afterward, we sat together and compared lists. We were pleased by how much they did not overlap. We attributed the lack of overlap to our distinct perceptions of our shared experiences and how we had individually applied those experiences to the marriage. We would say we were surprised at the lack of overlap, but as you'll read later, we often have different takes on just about everything from whether nuts belong in brownies to the proper way to load a dishwasher so no real surprise there… But we digress. Reviewing our items together was a walk down memory lane as we discussed the events and stories that resulted in each lesson. Some lessons were obvious to both of us, and some required explanation, but it wasn't difficult to get on the same page about each of the items.

In the end, we were able to create our consolidated list and that gave us the outline for who would write which section.

During the stream, Clarence presented the lessons he wrote about and Yalonda hers. And that is exactly how we present them here in this book. You'll read some in Yalonda's voice and some in Clarence's while others reflect our joint thoughts. Some of what we discuss are principles we live by daily, and some are light-hearted and jovial but lessons nonetheless. Some are simply practical, but all are important to the health of our marriage in some form or fashion.

A single thread you'll find woven through several chapters is the topic of communicating when we disagree. Why does it take several chapters to discuss what we've learned about communication? Because we often hear that communication is **THE KEY** to a lasting relationship. But, almost just as often, we don't hear about the details on communication. In our experience, rarely do couples openly discuss the specifics of the scenarios where communication is most difficult. We don't want to pry, and we don't want to overshare our own struggles, but shouldn't we talk about this more? There are so many facets of communication to explore. For example, how do we say the hard but necessary things to each other and keep the relationship intact or even improve it? When should we just shut up? When should we consider revisiting the topic after we've had sex first? What? Yes, we said it. Sex first, then argue. But we'll get into that later.

We recognize that every marriage is different and that there are people from so many walks of life that we could never begin to cover it all here, but the response to our anniversary stream underlined for us the fact that we can all learn from one another. Even if you are learning from another couple what **not** to do, you've learned something.

As you read, you may chuckle as you relate to parts where you recognize your relationship or yourself. But it's also cool if you laugh and say, "Nah this isn't us at all." No matter your response, we hope that some part of this book will be a catalyst for conversations between you and your significant other about what you value in your relationship, what you want to do more of, what you want to change, or what you may not have considered before now.

We put in a lot of work to become the co-functioning unit we are today, and we recognize it doesn't stop there. As we go forward, we'll be required to rework things we thought we'd already worked on, and we'll be required to take on new work we couldn't have anticipated based on the previous work. (See how many times we used the word 'work' here?) But when you're in a marriage with someone who is also doing the work right beside you, the work is worth it. The work results in life-long joy and companionship.

If you're looking for a book about how to find or be the perfect mate, this isn't the one. But if you're ready for a little messiness mixed in with commitment then please join us on this tour of key stops along the journey that was our first 25 years. We're happy to have you.

Thanks in advance for taking the time and we hope you enjoy it!

Track 1

Ain't No Stopping Us Now

Clarence and I like to work on stuff together. Rather, Clarence and I would like to work on stuff together. Rather, I would like to work on stuff with him if he would do things the way I do them, and he would like to work on stuff with me if I saw things the way that he does. At least that's the way it seemed early on in our marriage. We are both the eldest child in our respective families, and that meant we both were used to being entitled to tell others what to do and how to do it.

Raise your hand if you know that's a recipe for disaster in a marriage. Well, maybe not quite a disaster, but we certainly faced our share of disharmony when we needed or wanted to tackle tasks together.

For example, we're in love and we believe in sharing household duties. We've just had a lovely dinner, let's stand side by side at the kitchen sink and do the dishes together. Sounds like a Hollywood love story, right? Not quite…

Remember, we were both leaders among our siblings before marriage. So what would be a romantic movie scene that starts with him gently dabbing soap bubbles off of my nose before I playfully snap the dishtowel at his perfectly taut butt cheeks and ends with him carrying me up the stairs for some well-earned lovemaking, is actually more like a sitcom scene where I'm correcting his [air quotes] "obvious" kitchen-cleaning blunders, and he's frustrated with me redoing his work. It sounds something like this:

> Me: What do you mean you don't rinse the food off of the dishes before putting them in the dishwasher?
>
> Him: What's the point of using a dishwasher if you're going to wash the dishes first?
>
> Me: What are you going to do when a pea gets stuck in the mechanism again and the dishwasher stops working?
>
> Him: That's why we pay a home warranty premium, so they can send someone to fix it or replace it if needed!
>
> Me: We won't need to get it fixed again if we'd just use it the way it's supposed to be used in the first place!
>
> Him: How much of your life do you want to spend pre-washing dishes?
>
> Me: *silence*

Him: *silence*

You get the picture.

What we eventually grew to realize is that I was better at seeing the trees, while Clarence keeps his eye trained on the whole forest. In other words, I'm more detail-oriented and interested in making sure each tree and limb is evenly spaced and coiffed. So much attention to detail and desired perfection can make reaching a project or task's finality a long and painstaking process as I edit and re-edit. Clarence, on the other hand, keeps his eye on the goal and gets us to an end-product much more quickly, though we often need to revisit and tighten up some of the details once he's done. We've learned to view each other's approaches not as individual deficits to the process but as complementary pieces. When we combine our strengths, we create something better than what either of us could make alone.

We finally figured out how to value and apply each other's strengths so that they supplement one another and so that each of our weaknesses are mitigated. With the overall goal of the project at the forefront, and the details well attended to, we get a much better end-product than if we had chosen one way over the other. We get there faster because we save all that time arguing over how to do it "right." And we also get there happier with each other and with each person's contribution.

Track 2

Pick Up the Pieces

Clarence and I being together is the quintessential example of the natural law that opposites attract. He is an extrovert – a gregarious and unreserved person who enjoys and seeks out social interaction, while I am an introvert - most relaxed in my personal space. Look up *Signs You May Be an Introvert* on WebMD, and I tick all the boxes. He values confrontation, and I would avoid all conflict if I could. I take time (sometimes days) to process my response to an argument, while his response is ready before I even finish my statement (or so it seems). He loves his PB&J an inch thick, and his foods dripping with sauce, while I meticulously spread the PB as thin as construction paper and often take my sauce on the side.

And as with just about everything else, we have very different working styles and often us trying to work on a task together would end in discord and disunity (see Track 1).

Even though we are such opposites, we love to be in each other's space and do stuff together and, as mentioned in Track 1, our consistently opposing approaches to tasks would be maddening. We'd try to sit together and work simultaneously, but we'd bump against each other constantly. The plan would be to pay the bills together or write a joint email, and our intimate working situation would quickly deteriorate to "Why are you doing that first?" or "Doesn't it make more sense to add this now?" or "This is going to take forever if we do it this way!"

At the onset of a task, one or both of us would happily make the adjustments our spouse asked for, and then eventually we would make them begrudgingly until by the middle of the process we were snapping and scoffing angrily at each other. Finally, one of us would exit, often before the work was done, and the one left working was as likely to feel abandoned as they were to breathe a sigh of relief.

So while, as described in Track 1, we learned to value the strengths of each other's different styles, we also had to realize that, for the sake of the marriage and our sanity, we should divide the tasks, work separately, and then bring the separate parts together.

I'm not really sure how long we endured these struggle sessions before we started dividing tasks or who was the first to suggest it but thank God for whenever we did and however it came to be. Now, the way we make potato salad is the way we do life together. He knows that dicing the vegetables is the part of the process I least enjoy, so any time potato salad is on the menu, he preps small bowls of finely diced onion, green pepper, and celery for me. I happily jump to boiling the potatoes and eggs and then advance to the fine art of combining all the ingredients in the perfectly right amounts. Our potato salad is part "him" and part "me" just the way God intended. Shout-out to my mother-in-love Pat for her awesome recipe and technique! It's part "you" too Trici!

So many of our tasks and accomplishments as a couple are part him, part me. Getting the kids ready for school in the mornings – I get them dressed and he feeds them. Helping my son apply for college scholarships – he researched the programs and I helped my son complete the applications. Writing this book! As you can probably tell, some of the tracks are by him and some by me. We both edited all of them. Lord knows if we'd tried to do them together, the chance of it seeing the light of day would have been slim to none. Not to mention, the 25th anniversary might have been our last!

Track 3

Deep Waters

Not everything you learn while married is an epiphany; sometimes you are just reminded of the simple things. Things you might have learned as a child but forgot. Then, through a series of unexpected events, the two of you share an experience that brings one of those early childhood lessons to the forefront of your mind. This is the truth in our case, and it has become a staple of our relationship.

In 2000, after finishing graduate school in NC (go Heels), we got a great opportunity to live and work in Zurich, Switzerland for 6 months. I worked for UBS Bank and Yalonda at the University of Zurich. Our goal while we were there was to travel as much as possible.

We worked all week, and then met at the main train station on Friday afternoons to take the trains to various cities and countries over the weekend. We had it all planned out and we killed our plan. We went to Venice, Milan, Paris, Nice, Munich, Rome, and so many more exciting cities. It was great! It was everything we'd hoped for.

One of the major things we observed during our travels was that Europeans like all their drinks served at room temperature. It was bad enough when we couldn't drink the water in some of the places we visited but add to that the fact that it was summertime and whatever we drank was room temperature. It was the worst! We complained to each other about this almost every time we ate out. Sometimes we would ask for ice for our drinks and they would look at us as if we were making a ridiculous request and then reluctantly give us only 2 or 3 small cubes. It was as if there was some sort of ice shortage. Just absolutely crazy to us and one of the hardest cultural differences to get used to.

On our very last trip, we decided to fly rather than take the train because we found a cheap last-minute special on a flight. We flew from Zurich to Tunis, Tunisia for a 3-day weekend. *Side note: This was all pre 9/11, so flying was much simpler in those days. Remarkably, the Tunis airport was the first place we ever saw police officers carrying automatic weapons, but that's a story for another time.* Once we landed, we grabbed a cab from the airport to a beachfront town called Hammamet. We checked into our hotel, the Bel Azur Thalassa, and it was the best hotel we had stayed in our entire time abroad. AND the prices were incredible. For roughly $85 a night, our room included access to 3 private pools, a volleyball pit, a game room, a private beach, and 3 all-you-can-eat meals every day. We were in heaven.

During our first night at dinner, while we were enjoying our meal, I glanced at the table next to us and noticed something shocking. There was an entire *bucket* of ice on the table. I tapped Yalonda and pointed to the bucket and we were both drooling like Wyle E. Coyote. We hadn't seen a bucket of ice since leaving the U.S. We got our waiter's attention and inquired about the bucket. He said they were available upon request. Elated by this news, we asked him to bring us a bucket AND a couple of Cokes too, because this was cause for celebration! Yalonda was pregnant with our first child so vodka on the rocks wasn't an option. We toasted the night away like those sodas were Dom Perignon. During every meal for the rest of our trip, we continued the same celebratory drinking and living in the euphoria of drinking sodas the way God intended them…. COLD. After 3 days, our vacation came to an end and we flew back to Zurich on cloud nine.

On Monday morning at work, I started getting the worst stomach cramps I've ever experienced. They would come and go every couple of hours, but they were getting progressively worse. Then I started having to frequent the bathroom. Things didn't reach the level of diarrhea, but I was making #2s way too often. Early that afternoon, my office phone rang and it was Yalonda. She was experiencing similar symptoms and hers were much, much worse. So much so that she went to the ER to get checked out. They ran some tests and sent her home. She started feeling better by late Tuesday. My symptoms persisted longer, even though they were never as severe. Finally, on Wednesday we got the results of Yalonda's test from the hospital. She had contracted a bacterial infection typically associated with drinking unclean water. When she told me, I couldn't believe it. We only drank bottled water and even used bottled water to brush our teeth. How could we get Montezuma's revenge? We thought and thought. Then it came to us. ICE IS WATER!!!!!

Track 4

My Little Love

Parenting is easy …said no actual parent ever. Am I right?! We haven't even mastered the marriage relationship yet, and we go and bring new people into the mix. People who totally depend on us and spend half the time thinking they know better than us. We make these brand new humans, and it's our job to raise them to adulthood, but there is no advanced training for the particular individuals that we are dealing with. It's all learn as you go and trial and error. We also want to still recognize ourselves once our kids have become adults. How do we parent effectively while still retaining the sense of ourselves that we've become accustomed to? Raising the unique humans we are given can challenge us to the core of our being, including what we believe, what we want to achieve, the lifestyle that works for us, and so much more.

In addition, it seems like God has quite an interesting sense of humor with the way he matches kids to parents. Some of us feel like we are parenting ourselves based on how much our kids are like us. And, yes, maybe they have some of our most highly valued traits. But almost certainly they also have the characteristics we struggle with the most within ourselves and/or those of our spouse. Then there are those of us for whom it seems we are raising someone who couldn't possibly have gotten their genetic code from us. "Who is this foreigner I have nothing in common with?" we find ourselves asking.

Honestly speaking, some parents seem to be blessed with a natural astuteness, disposition, and discernment for parenting the children they have. In my opinion, many of the traits that make the best primary and secondary educators also make the "best" parents. Then there are some of us for whom parenting is more challenging. How we are prepared to parent is not exactly the best fit for the children we are charged with raising.

Like most new parents, while I was pregnant Clarence and I each imagined the type of parents we would be and we dreamt of the parent-child relationships we would have. We thought about all the traveling we'd do as a family and we were proud in advance of the citizen of the world we'd raise.

It wasn't long after our daughter was born that we began to get clues that our expectations for parenting (however realistic or unrealistic they may have been) did not match the child we were blessed with. Diagnosed with autism when she was just shy of 3 years old, she is severely affected by it as well as by an intellectual disability. As you might guess, while she is bright, affectionate, and has such an endearing smile and infectious personality, our journey raising her has been an atypical one to say the least. We could write a whole other book on that (and maybe we will).

Our son arrived when our daughter was about 3 1/2 years old. As even-keeled, good-natured, smart, and talented a kid as he is, again we eventually learned that some of our expectations were not in sync with our reality. For instance, Clarence has two brothers and they all played sports. His dad played sports as well. He had no experience with a kid like our son who is much more of an intellectual and an artist than an athlete. Clarence struggles with how to engage and bond with a boy whose personality and interests were and are so different from what he knows. At the same time, I had even less experience with boys because I grew up with all sisters for most of my childhood (my stepbrother lived with us for a few years when he and I were adolescents).

What we've learned is to raise the children that we *have* as opposed to the ones we imagined we'd have. This is no small or simple objective to achieve. At the same time that we are to be leaders, guiding and counseling our children to grow into fulfilled and balanced adults, we also have to be open to learning – learning from them and other sources of wisdom. And knowing which source of wisdom to learn from is also daunting because there are so many "expert" opinions on the subject.

But when we could set our expectations and predeterminations aside, pay close attention, and really see the wonderfully unique humans before us, every now and then we got glimpses into how to engage with them so that we could teach them and show them love effectively.

We had to be willing to admit when we don't know everything and apologize when we made a mistake. We had to realize that our children are not us and that sometimes what worked for us as children won't work for them. We had to understand that, and we are continuing to learn and be creative and resourceful. That doesn't mean at times we don't feel like we are in over our heads, like an exam we didn't study for but chose to take. The good news is that it's open book, open note, and we can talk. So, you just keep plugging away hoping you can get a passing grade but are unsure of the curve.

Parenting challenged our marriage relationship directly as well. Having kids basically tripled the opportunities for disagreements. We had to work hard to remain united, to support and respect one another as each parent doing their best, and to learn how to talk through our challenges to devise solutions we could both be happy with. Many of our marriage preservation tactics grew out of parenting together.

Now that our children are 21 and 18 years old, we can look back on the journey thus far and find so much to be proud of and rejoice over in our kids and in ourselves. At the same time, we recognize what we might have done differently if we knew then what we know now. We also know the journey isn't over, and we are gearing up for the next phase of parenting – launching independent adults. As with every other stage of their lives, for each of them, the launch will look very different. Pray for our energy, stamina, creativity, and resourcefulness, because we know we're going to need all of that!

Track 5

Tonight is Right

When I got married, I got all kinds of advice. But one of the areas where I got the least advice was sex. My parents' "sex talk" with me consisted of "don't do it, but if you do, protect yourself." I didn't talk with them beyond that. My dad showed me how to treat women in general and the importance of taking care of my family. My mom taught me about finances and how to pursue my dreams. She also said she didn't want to have to drive around to different homes to visit her grandkids.

"Have them all in one place," she instructed, "preferably with one woman." I took all these principles into my marriage and they have served me well. But no one ever talked to me about sex, and I learned quickly after getting married that even though it's such a vital part of marriage, it isn't the simplest part by far.

My experiences before marriage had led me to some conclusions about sex in general and how sex would be in marriage. I was totally wrong. Actually, "totally wrong" might be too extreme. A better descriptor is that my conclusions may have been *short-sighted*. I had been conditioned through movies and books to think that when I got married and settled down to be with one person I'd chosen for the rest of my life, something as natural and simple as sex would flow pretty easily. I mean at that point we had been intimate before so shouldn't it just automatically continue or even increase?

In the beginning of our marriage, we survived somewhat on raw energy, on the euphoria of our new commitment to one another. We were a little nervous, but excited, so sex came easily. Better stated, the desire to want to have sex was high so we prioritized it in our behavior. We were finally legitimate and any subconscious guilt we may have had was gone. We were free to do what we wanted, when we wanted, as often as we wanted! Exactly like I thought it would be.

But, over time, life started to catch up to us, (i.e., bills, a couple of kids, careers, etc.) and we found ourselves with competing priorities, pressures on our time, and our energy level was not the same. And we no longer had the luxury of sleeping in on the weekends to recover from the week because babies didn't know the definition of sleeping-in, the kid had an early game, the grass needed to be cut, one of us had to work, or the church had a function we had to attend. It began to seem like the demands on our time and energy had no end. Quality intimate time became more and more scarce and the frequency of sex began to fall off.

So what have I learned in 25 years of marriage? I've learned that if I want to get busy at 10 pm, I need to start at 10 am. I learned a key difference between men and women. Most men are great at compartmentalizing their lives. When we're at home, we're home, and when we're working, we are working. While engaged with one thing, we don't always think about other things. It took me 10-12 years to realize that wasn't going to work in my marriage because my wife does not compartmentalize this way. And it was never more evident than when it came to sex.

Fellas, if I want some lovin' at night, I have to let her know it's coming. I drop hints all day. Maybe I put a racy note in her purse or have lunch delivered to her office. Maybe I call or text her with hints about what I'm planning. Nothing crass (unless that's what she's into), but I drop small hints all day. If we're both working from home, I stop by where she is and rub the small of her back or squeeze her shoulders. I tell her I'm thinking about her and not just in a loving caring way, but in a naughty way. I'm not promoting nudes or sexting, but if that's what y'all do…do you. Maybe I bring her flowers home, take charge of preparing dinner, or wrangle the kids, all the while giving her that look. You know the look I'm talking about. Kiss her on the neck. Hug her tight. Tell her how good she looks. Put on my grey sweats. When we get upstairs, initiate the evening or just walk around naked. There are dozens of other ways to seduce her, but you get the point; love on her before you get to the bedroom.

None of these are hard to do, you just have to make a conscious decision and effort to do them. Let me tell you fellas when you get to bed, the faucet will be ON!!!

And ladies, this doesn't only apply to the guys. We need love too! Send a sexy text during the day. Let him know you're thinking about him. Let him know how you're feeling him, and you want to put it on him. When you finally get alone together, the mood will be set and action will ensue.

You're welcome.

Track 6

War of the Heart

At the beginning of our relationship, I was a woman of few words. I had always been a person of very few words, in just about every situation, and my marriage was no different. But I had married a man who had a verbal 500-word essay already prepared on any topic.

He had and has opinions, y'all. Opinions on opinions.

And some of them, in my humble opinion, were highly questionable and particularly debatable. But that didn't mean he wasn't fully convinced of them, didn't have paragraphs, headings, bullet points, and sub-points to support them, and couldn't speak eloquently on them like a Baptist preacher. I, on the other hand, didn't have practice speaking my mind. I knew my stance on many subjects but, as an introvert, putting my stance into words for an audience outside of my head wasn't a skill I practiced regularly, nor did I feel a need to. So, while I found myself having an inner reaction to what he would say to me, I didn't allow him in on it. In my mind, he would find out how I felt about it based on what actions I took going forward, not on what I said in the moment.

Like lots of married couples, we grew up in starkly different families with very dissimilar upbringings. That meant that many of the things each of us had learned to regard as the facts of life, were really just the facts of each of our own lives and upbringing and not to be accepted as universal truths. Looking back now, it's no surprise we disagreed so often. (Or was it that the same basic disagreements kept coming up repeatedly in different ways?) Needless to say, while some of his stances I found simply debatable as I said, there were plenty of instances where his words or actions infuriated me. But having grown up in an apostolic church, and with a preacher for a father, I was accustomed to being preached to and either saying amen in agreement or keeping it to myself if I disagreed. So there we were: Clarence pouring out his thoughts and opinions like a waterfall and me sitting still and silent like a glassy lake. As I've said, we've always been complete opposites, and this was just another arena where that truth was evident.

Having a wife of few words meant that if Clarence wanted to have an idea what I was thinking or feeling in the moment, he'd study my facial expressions like a biologist examining cells under a microscope. According to him, I don't give much there either. But when he'd say something I strongly disagreed with, he would jog something loose. More often than not, what would slip out from behind my stoic façade was a laugh. Not a guffaw, howl, or cackle; just a little chuckle. It wasn't planned. I wouldn't even realize I'd giggled until he'd ask, "Is that funny?"

Even when he pointed it out, I would deny it: "I am NOT laughing!" In my mind, there was no way I could have laughed because I certainly hadn't heard anything funny. Needless to say, the conversation, if I can call it that, would take a hard left from there. The laugh would allow me a release of the negative emotions and energy I was feeling and over time I started to choose to laugh in order to get that release. Eventually, I stopped holding in my thoughts and learned to share my disagreement effectively, but early on it was more just laughing and shaking my head.

Laughing was my response to the questionable points he'd make, i.e., the statements that just rubbed me the wrong way. However, when he laid down some infuriating sh… stuff – and I was already holding in my words, mad, hot tears would suddenly flow. Again, it was nothing that I decided or even wanted to do. But, I would be so frustrated and angry with him that I would have to cry to release it, or else I'd be compelled to cause him bodily harm. I would be upset with myself for crying so I'd cry harder, and then crying like a baby in the middle of an argument (where he was doing most of the talking anyway) would make me want to hurt him more.

I had the presence of mind not to give into my violent impulses. Sometimes I'd take out my frustration on a nearby countertop or pillow, or I walked away, but by God's grace and mercy, Clarence's life was spared over and over and he's still here today. So reader, please take my advice, if you have a wife who cries during an argument, hush your mouth and give her space. Because she's likely doing everything she can to not send you to your maker at that moment!

Track 7

Love Changes

One of the tough things about marriage is the ever-changing nature of people in contrast with the reluctance of people to change. It's a relationship paradox. Two opposing forces are acting on the marriage, and the marriage itself multiplies the impacts of the paradox.

You love certain characteristics of your partner. You love that they are funny, that they are responsible, that they are romantic, or simply how much they love you. You want those things to stay the same and never change. But, at the same time, you pretty much expect yourself and your partner to change in some ways over time – to grow wiser and better with life experience. You especially want the aspects of them you're not so fond of to change, but what if the things we hate about them never change?

If your spouse doesn't grow in a major area, like developing better financial management skills or losing their wandering eye, you might be facing a deal-breaker easily. But what about traits that have smaller impacts, like the fact that they rarely clean up after themselves, that they don't compliment your cooking, or that they don't call when they're out for hours. Maybe they talk too loud or too soft or too much. You get the idea. These are things you put up with when you were dating and then even during the early parts of your marriage. But now, after 5, 10, or 15 years of marriage, they drive you crazy!!!

Of course, you want them to change all of their less desirable habits or traits, but some of them you've learned to let go of or get over. Others you've complained about numerous times. You've let your spouse know how much they bother you and why. And still, you see little to no meaningful or lasting change. Eventually, you reach your breaking point and you wonder if it's worth it. You're so tired of picking up after them. You're tired of the endless shopping. You're tired of feeling unappreciated because they never tell you simply, "the food was good." You wish they wanted more out of life. It may seem small to them, but you begin to feel like you're going to go insane if this doesn't change and they don't do something about it.

So anytime I talk to couples considering marriage, I offer this piece of advice. Think about traits and behaviors you dislike about your partner right now that you don't consider a deal-breaker. Now think how your life will be with this person if they never change in that area. I mean NEVER. Would you still be able to make it work? If the answer is no, then it actually is a deal-breaker. If it's yes, then you have to accept the fact that the behavior might never change. I mean fully accept it. You can want it to change. You can ask for it to change. You can pray for it to change. But understand it may never change. It just might be too deeply ingrained in who they are.

Coming to this realization is a perfect place to take a few deep breaths and WOOSAH! WOOSAH!

Now that you've taken a few cleansing breaths with me, let me tell you what youhave to do (or at least what is working for me). You have to learn to change your re- sponse to the behavior in a positive way. This is the only thing you truly have control of. So rather than wait for a compliment about your food, ask "Did you like the food?" Maybe you buy something that holds their shoes and slippers by the front door so they don't leave them in the middle of the floor and let them know it's there. Maybe you learn to lean in more when they are speaking too low or tune them out when they speak too loud. None of this is meant to be manipulative of your spouse, only to lessen the impact of their behavior on you. It's about adapting to your surroundings because you recog- nize that sticking it out for the long term is more important than what happens in the short term. I recog- nized that change is a personal choice. One of the core principles that guide our marriage is that each of us sin- cerely attempts to put the other person's needs above our own. Consequently, we want to change the behaviors that displease the other person, even if those changes go against our natural tendencies.

People are fallible and prone to error, so you have to be prepared that they may never be able to change enough to satisfy your need for them to change.

That's the give and take of marriage. Even when we fall short, we work to show each other we care enough to keep try- ing.

Track 8

Insanity

It seems unnecessary to say, but throughout our 25 years, we have had some serious arguments.

Arguments where we were both furious with each other for whatever reason. Fortunately, our arguments have become fewer and farther between as the years have gone by, but when they do arise their intensity has not lessened. One of the unsaid principles we have lived by is not to go for the jugular in an argument. We have spent a significant amount of time with each other and have revealed some of our most personal and intimate secrets to each other. We've seen each other at our most vulnerable points and know each other's insecurities and fragilities. All that information is at my disposal during any argument. Should I use it to win the argument or should I refrain? What if I'm losing and I know saying this will prove my point? Off the top of my head, I say no, but the thought has or does cross my mind during the heat of the argument.

Some of us **need** to win. If you combine that with anger and personal knowledge, you have a recipe for an unfettered tongue. Remember, once you say it, you can never fully take it back. You can blame it on your temper. You can apologize. You can even make up. They can forgive you. But you can never "unsay" it and it won't be easily forgotten. Your relationship will be scarred. To what degree varies based on multiple factors like the subject matter, whether it happened in public or private, whether it's the first time, whether others were hurt by your statement, etc.

The very nature of a relationship involves conflict and conflicts can leave scars. But when privileged information is used in your arguments, you cut deep and leave deeper scars that are much harder to heal. Over time, they accumulate and enough of them will lead to the demise of your relationship or worse.

I asked myself a long time ago if winning the argument by any means necessary is worth the health of the relationship. There have to be some things that are simply off-limits. Either they are too personal, too private, or cut too close to the bone marrow.

Guard against letting a disagreement serve as an indictment of your spouse's character. For example, Clarence hates that I'm often running late. If he were to make his argument by asking "what type of person is always late?" or by calling me silly or shallow for being late, that's a character indictment that is hurtful and does nothing to solve the problem of my tendency to be late. To the contrary, if he says, "Babe, I'd really like to arrive on-time more often; what do we need to do to make that happen?" I can hear that as a legitimate request and a problem for us to potentially work together to solve.

We love one another. We have learned to remember that when we're angry. We certainly present our arguments, but we never forget that we love each other. We avoid going for the jugular.

Track 9

The Panties

In our bedroom, we have a dresser, a chest, and an armoire. In total, there are 17 drawers of varying depths and widths. Of those 17, I only have 3 drawers. I'm sure I'm not the only husband who has this kind of wife to husband drawer ratio, and I don't complain, but I do find one of my wife's drawers particularly hilarious. It's one of the largest drawers in our room and it's filled, top to bottom, back to front, and side to side with nothing but women's panties.

One day as I was washing my clothes, I realized the reason I was doing laundry was that I was out of underwear. Fellas, do you know what I'm talking about or is it just me? Either way, it occurred to me that she never runs out of underwear. NEVER!! So I decided to go in her drawer and count them just for kicks. I was astonished. She had 75 pairs of clean underwear in the drawer. *Insert explosion DJ drop right here.* Not to mention there were additional pairs in her hamper at the time. Incredible.

When Yalonda got home I asked her why she needs so many panties. She said a woman can never have too many pairs of panties. Is this true ladies? Fellas, did you know this? I purchase new underwear maybe once or twice a year. Combine those with the ones my mom buys me at Christmas (don't judge me), and I'm good. Yalonda went on to explain that there are so many different outfits and occasions and situations that women have to consider when getting dressed that she needs different styles of panties for each of them. She has bloomers, hipsters, thongs, high cut, French cut, control top, bikini, boy shorts, briefs, cheeky, g-strings (which are somehow different from thongs), and crotchless (ayyyyeeeeee), all in various fabrics like rayon, silk, cotton, and lace. Not to mention, she has a variety of colors in each style. And that's just the panties because you know she has a matching bra drawer. Say I again: Incredible.

My underwear decisions are much simpler - boxers or briefs. Color doesn't matter too much. I just want them to be comfortable, clean, and to not bunch. That's it.

So now I know that if I ever am questioning what gift I can give my wife, I can always scoop up a couple of pairs of panties. Either that or a subscription to SavageXFenty! #SupportBlackOwned

Track 10
I Give Myself Away

One of the relationship clichés I hear most often is "marriage is about compromise." Hearing this encourages couples to believe that conflict resolution is achieved through negotiation. I give a little, you give a little, and everything works out in the end. While I don't fully disagree with this, I think the premise is flawed.

The premise is that to be successful in marriage, you will have to give up some ground to your spouse. But you can rest assured that you will gain other ground in return. This is the foundation of compromise. But, in my opinion, there are situations where this is not an option. Sometimes you simply have to be willing to forgo knowing you will receive a return for the health of the marriage. My point is, in marriage, sacrifice is greater than compromise. I may agree to give up something and come away with nothing in the immediate term. That is not easy to come to terms with. Are you willing to give up what you feel your spouse should be reasonably able to do for you so that the relationship benefits? Can you make that sacrifice without holding a grudge against your spouse?

In our marriage, we have two major occasions where this principle played out, one for me and one for Yalonda. Both were very early in our marriage and one was 3 months before we got married.

Yalonda was raised Pentecostal Apostolic. I was raised in a mixture of Baptist and Catholic. Although both are Christian denominations, her faith had some very specific tenets that did not apply to what I knew or practiced, and I wasn't particularly religious anyway. We knew this when she accepted my marriage proposal in February 1996. For me, it wasn't a big deal, but for her, she was struggling with these differences and what they could mean for our marriage. A month or two into our engagement, she decided that if I didn't convert to Pentecostal Apostolic, she could not marry me. She did not want to enter into marriage "unequally yoked."

My first thought was to dissolve the relationship and move on. I wanted her in my life, but I also liked me just how I was. Why did I have to give up how I was living and what I believed simply to be with her? Could she not see the value in the person I was? She was asking me to give up what I had known and how I had behaved my entire life. If I didn't come to her understanding, she would not go forward with the marriage. If I did come to her understanding, I would be shedding a piece of myself that I valued. I had to decide if this was something I was willing to do. I was ready to break it off. She asked me to investigate my relationship with Christ for myself, to "try Him" so to speak before any decision. I did love her and I wanted to marry her, so I decided the relationship was valuable enough for me to at least try, so I did. We were not living in the same state at the time so I had to engage in the experiment on my own.

I started investigating the differences between our faiths. I began reading the Bible and attending church regularly (something I didn't do much of growing up). I was going to different churches all around Baltimore with friends and her family. I stopped drinking and cleaned up my language. We both became "born again virgins" and refrained from sex. I changed my entire outlook on my relationship with God, which at the time wasn't overly important to me, for the sake of my relationship with Yalonda, AND I'm so glad I did. What I learned during that period has proved invaluable to me as a man and a Christian. Learning that I knew Jesus but wasn't in a relationship with him changed my life.

The second major situation came 6 years into our marriage. We learned that our daughter was diagnosed with severe autism and we were having difficulty keeping adequate childcare. We also never knew when an issue would arise in school that would pull one of us away from our jobs. After much conversation and prayer, we decided it was in our best interest for Yalonda to leave her job for a while. It turned out that what we thought would be temporary ended up being permanent. Yalonda is one of the smartest women I know. She graduated at the top of her class in high school, she was awarded a full merit-based scholarship to college where she graduated cum laude in Biochemistry, and she was awarded a full scholarship to graduate school where again she graduated at the top of her class. Her first job offer was in her field doing what she had been trained to do. She was looking forward to building her career, but after only 2 years, she gave it up to support the needs of our family.

There was nothing I could give her in return for that sacrifice. But looking back, it proved invaluable in our daughter's growth and development. Yalonda was able to apply the research skills she had acquired getting her Master's to securing and engaging with our daughter's service providers. She created a village of people to support us, some of which are still in our lives years after. Yalonda has sat on panels and advised other parents on resources and treatments that are available for families of kids with special needs. She enhanced her resume by honing her existing skills and acquiring new ones.

Someone might say that either of us could have held the other in debt for the seriousness of the sacrifices we made. But that is our point here – when you're genuinely making a sacrifice for the relationship, there is no debt owed and there is no tit for tat. Some may point out that in the end, each of us gained immense value and experienced extremely positive outcomes as a result of our sacrifices. While true, neither of us knew what the outcomes would be when we decided to make the sacrifices. Looking back, I can see how for several years Yalonda's frustrations with her loss bubbled under the surface. Likewise, there were times I felt some resentment for the changes I made and what I felt I gave up. But in either of these instances, when each of us weighs the pros and cons, we rate our sacrifices as worth it to have the relationship we do now. If either of us had behaved selfishly, even if justified, the relationship as a whole might have suffered.

Our advice is this: as partners you have to honestly determine what your goals are for the marriage. If you want to be the best spouse you can be, that involves regularly asking yourself, "What can I do to make this marriage better for my spouse?" You don't stop asking because the answer changes as you both grow. But if both of you are seeking the answer to this question, then you'll find yourselves compromising more often than sacrificing and I think we can agree that's what we'd all prefer.

There are plenty of areas in a marriage where decisions to compromise or sacrifice arise. While everyone should deeply explore hot button topics like sex, money, religion, children, etc. before getting married, in all the excitement and emotion, we often don't do so adequately. And even when you have done so, your spouse is subject to change so yesterday's stance might not be today's stance and you may find yourselves reworking a previous agreement. In any case, when you and your partner can settle on a compromise then well done, but I'm cautioning that you at least have to be *willing* to sacrifice when needed.

If I could re-write the cliché it would say "Marriage requires compromise, but marriages that go the distance require sacrifice." You have to decide what you are willing to give up and what you aren't. Are you willing to give up something you want with the understanding that it may be a one-sided transaction in the near term? When you weigh the pros and cons, does a closer bond with your spouse outweigh the loss? So far, our answer has been yes and for that, I'm deeply grateful.

Track 11

Written All Over Your Face

I don't gamble and this is for 2 reasons. 1) I hate to give money away and 2) my face tells every thought in my head or emotion in my heart. If you suffer from affliction #2 like me and you're married, please pay attention to the following.

Did you know a polygraph (aka lie detector) works by detecting your physiological response to questions? They compare your body's response to the question to your verbal response because polygraphers know your mouth can lie, but your body? Not so much.

Like a polygrapher, Yalonda reads my body language and facial expressions as a telescopic view of my thoughts. When she asks me a question or asks my opinion on a matter, my face can't hide my private thoughts and she cares more about my thoughts than what I say. When my thoughts are positive, it's all good. But when they're negative or I'm holding something back, it is a problem. Maybe I'm being dismissive or simply disagreeing without verbalizing it. In either case, my face and body language betray me. Maybe it's just me, but I'm guessing someone reading this can relate.

I have to be honest up front. I don't have any solid advice on this matter. I'm still working on this myself. Here are a few approaches I've tried to communicate with Yalonda when I have negative thoughts and what I've learned from each:

- *I've tried simply telling Yalonda what I think* – This approach is a tricky one. When I was much younger and full of vigor, it got me mixed results. Sure, I got my point across, but she could take my straightforwardness as me being curt or insensitive, and this approach led to arguments and hurt feelings at times. She would also sometimes take me being straightforward as criticizing, condemning, and/or being aggressive. I think some of my responses early in our relationship led Yalonda to question and doubt herself too much. I had to learn that it is part of my responsibility as a husband to build my spouse. Saying things bluntly, no matter my intent, can be destructive and I don't want that. I've also learned that I am not right nearly as often as I thought I was. A little humility is something I've learned to have over time.

- *I've tried saying nothing* – I would do everything I could to hide my feelings from my face and say nothing. To prevent me from saying anything detrimental, I would say nothing and try to develop a poker face, erring on the side of caution. I found this tremendously hard, but it was doable, though not without consequences. Saying nothing is so outside of my nature that it HAUNTS me. Those unexpressed thoughts and feelings manifest themselves in other ways in my life. My stomach gets upset or I have trouble sleeping. My mind races, and I have to get it out. I play the conversation over and over again in my head. I lie down attempting, unsuccessfully, to fall asleep and look over at her sleeping like a baby. I wonder, how can you sleep when there's so much left to be said? Don't you know it's not resolved for me??? I can't tell you how many times I've awakened in the middle of the night, gotten out of bed, and written letters just to get the words out of my head. By the way, for me, this anxiety over unspoken thoughts is not just a marriage thing. It happens when I'm in any conflict. I've gotten better over the years, but I still have bouts of this. So since saying nothing to the person eats me up inside, I avoid it when possible.

- *I've tried asking her to listen to what I say, not to my body or tone* – Sometimes it works and sometimes it doesn't. In "Nonverbal Communication: How Body Language & Nonverbal Cues Are Key" Dustin Smith states that greater than 70 to 93 percent of communication is nonverbal, so I recognized that despite my desire for her to focus on my words, she is hearing more than I'm saying.

- *I've tried simply pointing out her options* – I have actively listened to what she says she is considering doing and offered alternatives. I back up my suggestions with anecdotes and references from my experience. Then I slowly turn away, leaving her with my words. I won't try to tell her what to do, just what I would do. This was marginally successful for a while until it wasn't. She figured out that my turning and leaving meant I didn't agree with how she planned to handle the situation, and she wanted to discuss why. That put me right back where I wasn't trying to be, so I no longer go this route.

- *I've tried picking my spots* – This is where I am now. Based on the lessons learned from everything I've tried, I am now better at reading the situation, reading her, choosing my approach, lying back, and letting it ride. Sometimes I can say what I think without the fire of my convictions so as not to appear aggressive or critical. I present information as suggestions rather than facts. Something as simple as saying "You might want to consider…." rather than "What you need to do…" could be the difference between a long-lasting argument and a successful interaction. Sometimes I just agree and support. Sometimes I stand strong in my convictions and say what I think and let the chips fall where they may.

I have grown to understand that there is honestly no single answer because, as I can see it, Yalonda is a moving target. She likely feels the same way about me. A friend said to me recently that women are not complicated, they are complex. Someone else said that women want to keep you on your toes lest you get bored. What I know is that for me, what may have worked yesterday may not work tomorrow. Yesterday's Price is not Today's Price! I'm learning to be okay with that and to roll with the punches. Kenny Rogers gave us the best advice many years ago. "Know when to hold 'em, know when to fold 'em, know when to walk away, know when to run."

Track 12

The Next Episode

Every relationship has some points of contention that take years to resolve or some agreed-upon rules of the relationship that fall off over time. One of the latter for us was whether or not one of us could watch the next episode in the series without the other. Yalonda's stance was if we start watching it together then we have to always watch it together. But with the hustle and bustle of work, kids, and overall family living, it got tougher and tougher for us to stick to this rule.

As we have discussed, at the beginning of our relationship, everything was all lovey-dovey and we did everything together. Every meal, every event, and even watching TV, we did together. Can't tell you how many

Sunday afternoons I spent watching movies about love-homicidal maniacs on Lifetime during the early years of our marriage —the glory days.

But over time, our schedules started to fill up with family matters and it became harder and harder to coordinate a time to do stuff together. One shared activity that was impacted the most was watching TV together. When she's free, I'm not, and vice versa. When we are free at the same time, we find better things to do than watch TV.

So after about 15 years of marriage, I made a decision. I decided I wasn't going to wait anymore for Yalonda to be available and ready to watch TV with me. I was going to watch whatever I wanted when I was free. I knew this was going to be super-controversial and potentially life-threatening, but I stepped out on faith!!

In the beginning, she got upset. "How could you watch it without me???" Then she would make me watch it again with her. I would agree to sit with her but I was usually on my phone or something.

Now, I know what you're thinking. If you didn't have time to wait for her in the first place, how do you have time to watch it twice? And you would be right, but this is a marathon, not a sprint! I wouldn't forego my long-term goals because of short-term losses. We were playing chess here, not checkers.

Over time, she stopped asking me because our schedules are so different and hard to coordinate. She got tired of trying to make it all work. So eventually, she started watching episodes without me because it was just easier.

CHECK-MATE!

So to all my fellas out there, let me give you permission to watch the next episode of The Walking Dead,

Abbott Elementary, or whatever show you want to watch without her. I release you! You may get some flak in the beginning, but it's okay. You're strong. You were built for this. You can handle it. It will be rough at first but, after a while, everything will smooth out and she will be watching TV without you like she did growing up. It's just a muscle she hasn't flexed in a minute.

Track 13
So Fresh So Clean

This is another one for the fellas. Because I grew up in a household with 3 boys plus my mom and dad, I had no frame of reference for how a girl behaves on a day-to-day basis until I got married. One of the things I learned that was shocking, hysterically funny, and an absolute turn-on is that women will clean naked. Who knew?

Now let's be specific. Sometimes my wife will go into the bathroom to shower. At some point, she determines the tub isn't clean enough for her to shower. Usually, by the time she makes this determination, she's already undressed and has the water running. So, without getting dressed, she will start to clean the shower before she showers. There's Ajax, Comet, and Clorox shower spray everywhere. (She's making me add here that the cleaners may be "everywhere" but none is on her.)

If she stopped there, I probably would have never noticed because that doesn't take very long; but she doesn't stop. Since she's already in cleaning mode, she just continues to clean. The toilet and the sink are next most times and if she's really being obsessive, she'll mop the floor. 15-20 minutes into her "shower," I'm wondering what's taking her so long. I ask, "What are you doing in there?" I come into the bathroom and see her standing there stark naked with rubber gloves on and cleaning products in her hand. The first time this happened, I thought, "What is going on here? Is this a kink?" but I never actually said it. I just started laughing. I eventually asked, "Why are you cleaning the bathroom naked?" Her answer was only, "It was dirty."

At the time I thought this may have been a one-time thing, but over the years I've witnessed this activity several times. It's now to the point where sometimes I purposely bust into the bathroom just to see if it's going on. Partially because I still can't believe it and partially so I can watch. I figure it's good for everyone. She gets her clean on and I get my peep show on! Please don't take this as a complaint. It is not. It is just an observation from a person who had never seen anything like that before.

When we did our broadcast for our anniversary, I told this story and was blown away by the number of women in the stream that admitted they do this too! Not one man co-signed this behavior…. NOT ONE. So for the fellas that don't know, hear me now, naked cleaning is a thing. Know it and enjoy it!

Track 14
Encourage Yourself

The only person responsible for my happiness is me. Full stop. End of sentence. Periodt. I cannot expect my partner to make me happy if I can't find happiness within myself and by myself. My spouse can learn my love language and use it to help me feel loved by him and to bring me moments of joy. My spouse can add to my happiness by being thoughtful, upbeat, and positive day-to-day, especially when I or we face problems. However, if I don't have happiness on my own, it is unfair of me to place the responsibility on him to do just the right things to overcome my unhappiness. It is an unrealistic expectation that can lead to me resenting him when he doesn't come through (because that is inevitable in this scenario) and/or him resenting me for the constant pressure and burden of my emotional state. If instead of nurturing my own internal and external sources of contentment (self-reflection, growth, hobbies, friends, etc.), I am counting on him and our relationship to be the one source, I am setting myself up for disappointment.

When our relationship was in its early years, the joy that comes from merely sharing experiences, loving words, laughs, or gifts could make me feel like these things would make me happy forever. However, inevitably, any discontent I had with myself before the relationship could be like an unchecked crack in a car windshield. If the glass has cracks, chips, or missing pieces, then the odds are that the entire windshield will shatter in a collision. It's best for me to fix the windshield's imperfections when they happen to help maintain its stability and integrity. Like damaged glass exposed to the pressures of winds and nature, a spirit of discontent only gets worse when the pressures of being in a relationship are applied.

If I depend on him as my sole source of happiness, or as more my source than I am, what happens when he is spent or busy or distracted? What happens when *we* are spent, busy, and distracted at the same time? (Hello, parenthood!) As you probably know, stress can sometimes make us humans abandon the new behaviors we've learned that nurture our relationship (such as those related to our partner's love language or necessary boundaries) and return to rudimentary, often less healthy, patterns of interaction (yelling, silent treatment, name-calling, selfishness). If there is an extended time of stress in our relationship, either or both of us are susceptible to not being our best selves. How then can I rely on him to be my source of happiness?

There are plenty of stressors in a marriage. Maybe your big stressor is money, your job, a sick parent, or dysfunctional family dynamics. For us, it's parenting. Allow me to tell you a little about that. When our daughter was diagnosed with autism, we were beginning to learn what that really meant in terms of how overwhelming her needs would be and the degree to which our parenting journey would differ from that of anyone we knew or had known. Simultaneously we were each going through one extremely challenging situation with her after another. I can see how there is an increased divorce rate among marriages with children with disabilities, especially with autism.

We really had to dig deep to be there for each other when things were the most difficult, especially when we didn't have any role models for parenting a child with her challenges and we were forced to depend on trial and error. I wanted to try A and he thought B was the way to go. We were both baffled and stressed and sleep-deprived, yet somehow we were also supposed to be responsible for each other's happiness? Hell, I could barely be responsible for the new human who was turning my whole world on its head. How could I also think about his level of contentment with life? How could he think about mine? We were just barely hanging on.

Now, hold on a minute. I'm sensing myself getting a little carried away as I write. Because, as I touch on elsewhere in this book, we should be able to trust that each of us has the other's best interest at heart, and that has to factor into our individual decision-making. And being stressed doesn't exactly absolve us of this crucial courtesy. It's a delicate balance that requires both of us to be on board and to be willing to let the other off the hook from time to time, with the understanding that I may need a pass now, and he'll need one later. It requires being aware of our own varying needs and capacities from moment to moment so that we can openly communicate those to each other. It requires us to constantly check in with each other, especially when a downward shift in mood is detected. Clarence and I often ask each other, "Are you okay?" or "Are we okay?" When the answer is no to either of those questions, I can be wide open to listen to what he has to say and be stable enough to listen and respond with kindness and genuine concern for his well-being and that of our marriage.

Ideally, it won't tear me apart to hear that he's dissatisfied or has been affected negatively by something I said or did. Ideally, we can work together to get us back where we want to be: joyful, in love, and strong together.

Track 15
Time Will Reveal

One of our friends who is always fashionably late says, "I'm never late. I get there exactly when **I** am supposed to." My college basketball coach used to say, "If you're on time, you're late." These are two very interesting perspectives on time management, and they perfectly describe the past 25 years of our marriage as it pertains to our 2 contending views on time.

Time management is one of those things that everyone has to learn at their own pace. Some of us are too rigid while some of us are too lax. Either way, everyone has some inherent tendencies that must be learned or unlearned throughout their lifetime. It's tough enough learning those lessons on your own, but it's doubly difficult when you are married, triply difficult when you and your spouse's time management approaches are vastly different, and exponentially difficult when you have kids.

In our relationship, I am the person who historically has emphasized time more rigidly, and Yalonda has been more relaxed with time. Early on, I could not understand how someone could be as dismissive and indifferent to time as she seemed to be. From my perspective, she didn't value time or certainly not the impact her time management had on others. Once, when Symone was a baby, we had to pick her up from daycare. The pick-up time was 6 pm. I asked if Yalonda wanted to go with me to pick Symone up. She said she wanted to go (you know how we can be as parents for that first child). At 5:30 she wasn't ready. I'm not sure why she wasn't ready, but I simply left. I'm not even sure I said anything. I just left without her.

In my mind, it takes 20 minutes to get to the daycare. If there's any traffic on the beltway, it could take 30 minutes. They charge $1 for every minute you're late. So 5:30 was the absolute latest we could leave and be comfortable knowing that we would avoid the late fee.

I'm not 100% sure why I left her without saying anything. We had been married for 6 years by this point. Looking back, I think I was a little tired of always waiting for her for what seemed like everything. I hated that feeling of having to rush to get to the destination or to get the item submitted or whatever. Whatever the reason, I'd had enough. Five minutes after I left, she called and we argued. Words were said.

Lots and lots of words.

I can't say that was the turning point in our battle to unify our views on time, but it was the beginning of multiple in-depth conversations surrounding the subject and defining what it was going to mean to us. While I won't begin to speak on how she processed those discussions, I can say that I began to make adjustments to both my thinking and my responses to "our time management." If I hadn't, this time thing might have become a deal-breaker for us.

Based on our discussions, I learned that she can get lost in time, feeling like she has more time than she actually does or things don't take as long as they actually do. However, more importantly, I learned she's not insensitive to this. There were times when she got frustrated by her time challenges even though I couldn't see her angst. I learned she wanted to change, but it just wasn't natural for her. As her husband, isn't it my job to help rather than disparage her for her weaknesses?

For me to help, I needed to first understand why she struggled with time. Not the symptoms, but the root. Through discussion and observation, I learned that she enjoys the present and **fully engages in it.** Anyone who has ever had a conversation with her knows this. When she's talking to you there's no doubt she's engaged: full eye contact, attentive listening, acknowledgments, the whole nine. There is no ticking clock of some future event in her head that is distracting her. At the moment, whatever is happening is exceedingly valuable to her and requires her undivided attention and effort. Those qualities are admirable and even though it has caused strife in our relationship, it doesn't diminish the value of these qualities. I didn't always understand that.

I, on the other hand, rarely lose track of time. There is almost always a running clock in my head. I know when we arrived, how long we've been here, and how long before we have to leave. No engagement supersedes the tick-tock of the clock in my head. This is where we are fundamentally different. I couldn't understand that this is not true for everyone. I judged her for not seeing things the way I do rather than understanding that everyone processes the world around them differently. Sounds silly to me now, but when I was young, I didn't have enough experience to understand how to see the world through someone else's eyes. Once I was able to empathize with her viewpoint and better understand my own, it was easy to put some tactics in place to help us better manage time together as long as she was willing, which she was.

My first adjustment was better managing our departure times. I know that in order to be on time she does the math from the time we need to arrive backward to the time she needs to start getting ready. So I save her some math by expressing out loud what time we need to leave to arrive on time. I figure out the drive time, accounting for traffic and parking, leaving her to do the math on what time she has to start getting ready to meet the departure time. As for me, I pad the departure time by 15 minutes. This gives me some peace of mind and she has some margin to work with.

Another adjustment we created was the use of signals to discreetly communicate with each other while we were out. Maybe I scratch my chin or touch the bill of my hat. Maybe she raises her single eyebrow – something I can't do although I wish I could –, but you get the point. We use subtle gestures to remind each other to check the time. Over the years, this has proven very effective because we have both grown together in this area a lot. It's gotten to the point where she now gives me signals way more often than I give them to her.

Finally, we've learned to exercise more patience and extend more grace to one another. Things are not always going to go on schedule. So I try to take a deep breath and relax. I don't jump all over her when she misses the mark. I've learned that she is quite aware she's running behind and consequently, her stress levels are pretty high. For us, emotions can run pretty hot when it comes to matters of time, and I suspect we are not the only ones. I try to calm myself, relax, and ask her what she needs from me. Maybe I can grab some shoes or a purse or put the bags in the car. I offer suggestions. Sometimes I just sit down and do nothing. She in turn doesn't jump all over me for trying to prod her along, understanding that I have anxiety around time and I'm only trying to help.

None of this is foolproof. We still have issues with how we manage time, but we are getting better and over the years the "bad incidents" have become much fewer and farther between. Her attention to time has increased greatly over the years, and I've learned that every event can't be part of a rat race. She's learned to be more attentive to time, and I've learned there is real value in being in the present and enjoying the moment, especially in social settings. We acknowledge each other's growth. Validation helps reinforce our feelings that we have made progress. When we falter, we try not to criticize, but rather offer feedback. Criticism is an emotional reaction and is often imprecise and harsh, while feedback gives the recipient actual information that they can use.

Our goal is not conformity, it is growth, together.

Track 16
Best Friend

Have you ever wondered about the out-sized, un-matched obsession men have with their "manhood?" I grew up in a house full of sisters, and it's certainly some-thing I had questioned. That is until I birthed a man-child into this world. Before then, I had little clue to how prominent a role boys' wee-wees play in their lives from the very beginning – literally from DAY ONE!

As a girl, unless you have a progressive mom or a commanding sense of curiosity, you may go through your entire childhood never knowing what your vagina even looks like! She's tucked away neatly and discreetly, inaccessible to her lady's eye at all times without a mirror and careful leg placement. You know she's there, and you learn through the years what she's for and how to take care of her, but she stays effortlessly in her hidden spot at all times. She could remain a visual mystery to her lady for their entire life if the lady so chooses.

Penises on the other hand?! A boy's penis is literally front and center even before his infant eyes have the capability to focus to see it. Little Johnson is a prominent soldier, marching to his own beat, daring his captain to defy or ignore him. Your son is never alone as long as he has Little Johnson. Long before it has anything to do with sex, Little Johnson is his first best friend, his ace, always there, as accessible to the eye as it is to the hand. Raising my son explained a thing or two about the boys and men I had known and their baffling sense of, shall I say, direct connectedness with (and obedience to in some cases) their Johnsons. Is it just me, or can other moms of boys also attest to this phenomenon? I know I am limited in my ability to explain the connection.

When we discussed this on our Twitch stream, I attempted to compare how early a man's relationship with his penis starts to that of an arm – meaning from the start, it's unmistakably there and has lots of uses. As soon as this statement left my lips, a man rapidly fired in the chat. "It's nothing like an arm," his words simply read, but in those 5 basic words, and with the speed he'd typed them, I could sense him stressing the absolute inadequacy of my comparison. Clearly, he was offended that I had compared his beloved Johnson to a lowly arm! I guess I have a little more to learn. He went on to say that the first best friend analogy was a much better fit because an arm you can live without, but not your "Day One" best friend!

Track 17

Solid

In my experience, trying to prove ourselves right in each and every disagreement, no matter how small, is a no-win situation. Yes, you may get your spouse to acquiesce to you, but is acquiescence really what you want? Or are you truly yearning for mutual understanding? Could there be a way that what we are going through can help us learn something new about each other or know each other more deeply? For example, a spouse may learn that their partner always felt excluded as a child from family decisions, and that's why they are adamant about holding regular family meetings. Or maybe one spouse grew up in a very controlling environment so now they're determined to give their kids more autonomy over aspects of their lives. When hubby and I aren't on the same page about something, do I want to be right or do I want to understand his reasoning in the situation? What was he trying to accomplish with the choice he made? How can we reconcile our individual objectives to reach a shared goal?

Every day, Clarence shows me he loves me with his actions. And every day, I'm choosing to respond with love and trust. And vice versa. Because of this consistent state of our relationship, even when he does something I don't like, I'm choosing to trust that it wasn't done maliciously. Even the person who loves me and whom I love can have *moments* (as opposed to patterns) of thoughtlessness, selfishness, or stress-response behavior. And in those moments I choose to believe his track record – the record that's shown that he wants the best for me and our relationship. When I am hurt, disappointed, or a need is going unmet, I express these feelings in love, trusting him to listen in love. We prioritize preserving the relationship, each other's spirits, and dignity above proving who's right and who's wrong. And because we're both invested in the relationship going the distance and it being a source of joy and elevation for each of us, we each take the other's issues seriously and work on becoming better.

We can't squander that level of trust and vulnerability by being petty. We've learned to choose our arguments carefully so that time spent in conflict is worthwhile. Do I need to point out every time I have to rinse his soap residue out of the shower or remove his sweatshirt from the living room? Does he need to say out loud everything that I do that he doesn't like or has asked me not to do? Do we engage in petty contentions or productive discussions?

We're going to choose arguments wisely and we're going to extend mercy for those things that are hardest to change when it's evident that the work is being done. In situations where necessary change is extremely difficult, counseling for one or both of us may be in order. In instances of everyday annoyances and differences of opinion, we disagree, but we choose to do so in love like 1 Corinthians 13. We treat each other with patience and with kindness. Neither of us demands that we get our way, and we don't dwell on what's happened in the past. Our goal is to preserve the relationship over being right.

Track 18

Baby Be Mine

Ephesians 4:26-27 says, "In your anger do not sin: Do not let the sun go down while you are still angry, and do not give the devil a foothold." Most of us get married trying to hold ourselves to this literal standard because we've heard it or read it. As a 25-year vet of marriage, I can say with absolute certainty that trying to abide by the literal meaning of the scripture is a tremendously stressful approach to problem resolution in marriage. Early in our marriage, I wanted to be a great spouse who didn't let problems linger, so when we had an issue, I would keep pounding and pounding on it trying to come up with a solution. I didn't realize how much I was pounding on Yalonda. I figured if we kept talking we could come to a resolution. Although I considered my intentions noble, it was very detrimental to our early marriage and even more detrimental to her.

Over time, I've evolved to believe we are misapplying the spirit of the scripture. The scripture is not directed at issues or conflict resolution, it's directed at us individually, instructing us to learn to quell our anger instead of letting our anger control us, marinating over days, festering into resentment.

In marriage, you will encounter many circumstances and situations that can put tremendous stress on you, your spouse, and the marital bonds. We all recognize the big stressors like kids, money, jobs, or issues with family members. But more often it's the mundane, day-to-day stressors like dirty dishes, a favorite item of clothing ruined in the wash, or a new jar of Jiffy in the pantry when you know I like Peter Pan that cause some of the most heated and/or frequent arguments.

Multiple times during the last 25 years, one of us has been absolutely livid with the other. We both have held strong opinions of how things should be, and like in any relationship, strong opinions can collide often and loudly. I remember once, in my arrogant youth, I told Yalonda that her opinion was wrong. SMH. Oh, how the naiveté of youth can betray us. New marriages are like young children in that they are constantly in need of attention and nurturing. Combine that with immaturity and you are bound to make these types of mistakes. What we had to do was learn how to grow **together** regardless of how we had grown up **individually**. We learned it takes time and wisdom to learn how to formulate your thoughts and communicate them effectively so that your partner understands, let alone come to a resolution. When we were young, I didn't understand that resolving issues is more of a process than a singular discussion that has to be solved before you fall asleep.

Let's get back to my original point. There have been times when we have been unable to resolve an issue between us and have simply gone to bed angry. Our way of maintaining connectedness even though we may be angry is touch. I may touch her leg with my foot or she rests her hand on my back. It's our way of saying to each other, "Even though I'm angry with you, I'm not going anywhere and we will get through this." We find that sometimes a good night's rest helps us calm our thoughts enough to have a productive conversation the morning after. Never underestimate the value of a good night's sleep.

Over the years, we have learned other things to do to help put us in a better space for effective communication. Exercise is the number one stress reliever for both of us. We don't have the energy to continue to be all mad when we've just worked out. Another is spending time with friends who have great energy. Hanging out and laughing are amazing relaxers.

We even stumbled upon a place outside of the house for us to have difficult conversations. When we were young and lived in North Carolina, we went to eat at K&W Cafeteria one day, and we found ourselves having a heart-to-heart and resolving an issue we were dealing with at the time. From then on, anytime we needed to talk, one of us would say, "Is it time to go to K&W?" It became a designated place for hashing out an issue. The food and atmosphere weren't important, and we could focus on the conversation. So much can be ironed out over a good meal. Finally, I can't leave out sex and physical intimacy as stress-relieving activities. We'll talk about that in Track 22. I'm certain pillow talk has prevented wars.

The point is often you have to quell your anger long enough to have a real conversation about the issue you are facing. As we discussed throughout this book, you have to be open to listening to the other person's point of view and seek to reach understanding as opposed to proving your point at all costs. You can't do this while you're angry so it helps to figure out strategies to mitigate your anger. I'm not at all saying it's easy, but you must strive to reach the place where you can have dialogue, reassure your spouse that you are here to stay and that you believe you will get through this. …even if you don't know how at the moment.

The goal of the scripture is sound and profound, but the practical application of that principle requires you to be less literal and more introspective. Going to bed angry is not the worst thing you could do. Feeling so justified in your anger that you hold onto it, nurture it, and allow it to motivate your actions is much worse.

Track 19

Concentrate on You

I really, really enjoy spending time with my spouse. – Wait, was that too many reallys? Because actually, every now and then, it's not all that enjoyable. – Anyway, I know we both have these feelings. "Come with me while I do this" is a request heard often between us. Even after our many years together, when one of us leaves the house, that one will call the other from the car – sometimes staying on the phone until the destination is reached. We can talk about anything, from someone else's baby to the latest nonsense on social media to politics to TV shows/movies. We hang out in the kitchen. We hang out in the bathroom. And I do mean hang out in the literal sense. One of us will sit at the vanity while the other takes a shower. We often grocery shop together, go to the movies, and, almost by necessity, take our daughter on outings together almost every weekend. We love and value each other's company.

It all started when, after we got married, Clarence moved to North Carolina to live with me while I was in school. I was a student there when he proposed, and he was willing to pick up everything and join me to start our life together. We've often looked back over that time and recalled how all we had was each other. We did not have any family or close friends that lived within 200 miles (except, of course, the new associates we made while there). And, in retrospect, we realize that with most of our friends either single or early in their marriages them-selves, it turned out to be such a blessing that we had to fully depend on each other. There were no parents' or friends' homes that we could run away to when times were difficult. And, boy, did we experience some pretty tough times in the first two years of our marriage. There was no "bro" or "sis" who would snatch one of us away when we got on each other's nerves or sit in our kitchen and give us advice that may or may not help. There was no one to occupy the time that we needed to spend with each other.

We also didn't have our first child until we had been married for over four years. So during the "formative" years of our marriage, we were able to concentrate on ourselves as a unit. Splitting chores, paying the bills, man-aging time, making decisions, traveling around the world – those were the marital habits and more that we were developing and practicing. We made quite a few mistakes as we were learning how to relate to and depend on each other during those years, but we did it on our own for the most part, with minimal involvement from the peo-ple who knew us when we were single. There may have been a few phone calls here and there (long-distance charges still existed in those days), but the distance from our friends and family made a huge impact on us growing together. One of the most valuable benefits was developing that love of each other's company that I spoke about above.

But while we are each other's favorite conversationalists, travel, and hang-out partners, I am not interested in everything that he is interested in, and vice versa, and we have learned that it doesn't help either of us to feign interest when it's not there. It feels right for him to have some time to go play golf with his buddies or for me to go to the New York Wine and Food Festival with my sorority sisters. He can watch football while I read a book. He can watch his Blaxploitation and sci-fi fantasy shows, and I'll watch my dramas and sitcoms. For stress relief, he'll DJ and I'll pull out my dumbbells and get in a strenuous workout. We each can periodically travel or go out for a meal without the spouse. (He doesn't prefer to travel without me, but Lord knows, I need my girls' trips and girls' nights out!)

In these ways, we separate, enjoy our time apart, and come back together replenished and ready to pour into each other and our relationship again. As much as we love spending time together, we appreciate the opportunity to miss each other, and to have new stories to tell when we're back in the same space. We grow by granting each other the room to follow pursuits that the other may not be interested in. Then we share so that we can each enjoy the other's experiences vicariously. We want each other to get joy from other sources, then when we are in the same space again, our collective joy has now been raised by his new joy multiplied by mine. Sounds a little strange and corny to me to write it like that, but it's true!

Track 20
Talk to Me

In long-term marriages, you get to know each other extremely well over the years. You learn each other's likes and dislikes, moods, and mannerisms. You learn each other's tendencies and how your spouse typically responds in specific situations. The longer you're together, the more information you amass, and the better you understand your partner. Or at least that's what you think.

Muhammad Ali once said, *"The man who views the world at 50 the same as he did at 20 has wasted 30 years of his life."* This has never been truer than when it comes to relationships and marriage. So often we feel like we know our spouses so well that we "know know" them. Even down to believing we know how they are going to respond to specific questions. We can be so confident that we pose the questions and hear the responses **all in our heads**. Sometimes we are having full-blown conversations with ourselves. You think, when I say this, they are going to say that. And you continue this back and forth until you come to a conclusion on what you're going to do or not do based on a conversation you've had with yourself. If you think about it, that's just plain crazy.

I've even gotten angry at Yalonda for her responses to conversations we've never actually had. I'm sure she can say the same thing. I'm sure YOU can say the same thing. All upset over a conversation you had with yourself. Sounds silly when you say it like that. Getting mad at the other person based on the response you're so sure they would have said but never actually said.

Experience has taught us that we shouldn't have the conversation in our heads, we have to verbalize it. Allow the other person a chance to show you their growth. Regardless of how many times your assumptions have been correct, you have to give them a chance to surprise you.

In the biblical parable of the persistent widow (Luke 18:1-8), the widow continually asks for justice against her opponent from the judge. The judge is characterized as uncaring. The Bible doesn't say how many times she petitioned the judge; it just says she was persistent. Eventually, her persistence got the judge to grant her requests. Surprise! When discussing this in church, we tend to focus on the widow getting her request through her persistence. I would like to focus on the growth of the judge. He grew and changed. Not necessarily because he wanted to but because the case was presented to him so many times. She likely didn't make the same points or argument every time, but her goal was always the same, to convince this judge to rule in her favor.

The widow could have resigned herself to believing she knew what the judge's answer would be. He'd turned her away numerous times before. She could have argued in her head but she didn't. Honestly, I'm not sure what I would have done in her position, but she kept verbalizing her request and her persistence eventually swayed the mind of a person who cared nothing for her. Imagine what it can do to someone who loves you.

This is not a license to harass or nag your partner. It's just a plea to make your requests known to one another. People who love one another have been known to do some of the most selfless and amazing things for each other when given the opportunity. But, if you don't have the conversation, you will never really know.

Track 21

Love is a Battlefield

How do you and your spouse argue? Is one of you likely to walk away hurt? Is there typically a winner and a loser? Are you in full armor with battle shields up and swords out? Are accusations thrown like daggers? "You always…," "You never…," or "I'm the only one who…" Are past mistakes resurrected from the shallow graves of previous arguments and conscripted into the fight? If this sounds familiar, then you know that regardless of who wins or loses, it costs you both a lot. Eventually, you call a temporary truce and you each retreat to treat your wounds alone. Your partnership, your love, and your trust for one another have been battered and bloodied, and you don't know if it will survive another assault.

Or maybe you've decided that it would be better to avoid arguments altogether. When disagreements arise, do you simply clam up? Do you have an internal dialogue where you process the situation without your spouse and arrive at your own conclusion instead of having a dialogue **with** your spouse where you work together to resolve your differences and determine how to move forward?

Neither of these two extremes – battling or refusing to engage at all – are healthy for a relationship that you want to last. Can a relationship survive if spouses treat each other as enemies to be conquered, detractors to be maneuvered around, or rivals to compete against? How much stronger and more durable is a relationship where each spouse respects and values the other as an ally?

What does allyship between spouses look like? Do you recognize that you each come to the marriage with different, yet valid, experiences? Do you value each other's perspectives? Do you seek to understand where your partner is coming from? Do you consider how their viewpoint adds value to every situation? Do you acknowledge that you are on the same team, both desiring success for your family, even when you disagree for the moment on how to achieve it? Are you committed to the longevity and prosperity of your relationship? Do you trust that your spouse is committed also? Do you want the best for each other?

This is the armor that Clarence and I have learned to carry with us into our arguments. We no longer need armor to protect ourselves from each other, but to protect the relationship against our egos and opinions. No matter how strongly we disagree about something, in the end, we want the relationship to last through the disagreement. Not just last, but get stronger if possible. We strive to use a disagreement as an opportunity to reach a deeper understanding of one another.

This is not easy for us. As you well know by now, Clarence and I are total opposites in so many ways. We know that we often have differing opinions based on our separate backgrounds and experiences and that neither of our opinions is "wrong." An opinion may seem right or wrong because of how it lines up with or goes against your experience, but the real test of an opinion is its impacts and consequences. Is it benefitting you or helping you make the progress you want to make? If not, then it doesn't make the opinion wrong per se, but it does make it unhelpful for your current situation. What is the best way to view the situation based on your joint experiences?

We've also learned that often it's vital to ask for or to grant each other the time to process what has been said or what has occurred to develop a thoughtful and deliberate response. When you react immediately in the heat of the moment, it's easier to say hurtful or exaggerated things that you can't unsay later. Take a beat. One of us will say, "I need time to process this. Let's please discuss it later." The key is that you have to get back to them, and you have to do it relatively soon. As days go by, there is more time to ruminate, and it looks like you don't care enough to reflect and circle back. But when you come back to them ready with a thoughtful and transparent response, you keep the door open for fruitful dialogue.

Track 22
Pillow Talk

I came to a marriage-altering realization about 5-10 years ago. I wish I had realized this sooner in our marriage, but such is life. I finally realized the power of sex in a relationship, especially when you have reached an impasse in an argument. Now there are a bunch of women out there who have already realized this I know. I was a little slow on the uptake. I would think to myself, "I'm mad at him, and he is not getting any until we resolve this!" You know how Jay Kyle was on My Wife and Kids: The first thing to go when Michael was acting up, was "aaaall-uh-dis," she'd declare as her body rolled and her hands gestured an outline of her silhouette. That was me in a nutshell without the dramatizations. And when there was tension between us, the silence and distance could last for days. I'd hold in everything I had to say, mulling it over and over in my head and imagining his negative responses to justify my not giving him a chance to respond. Eventually, the promise we made to preserve our relationship would win out and one or both of us would finally relent and talk about what was bothering us.

Honey, that was lost time that we'll never get back. Time that could have been spent enjoying one another, strengthening our connection as a couple, and building each other up. Instead, there was a wedge between us. A wedge that I've since come to believe a significant portion of which was due to me being so willing to take sex off of the table. It wasn't the only factor, but after I learned to prioritize physical intimacy differently, I saw the positive impact it had on our ability to communicate more freely and get issues resolved more quickly.

But before I started looking at things differently, I read a book by Shaunti Feldhahn called *For Women Only: What You Need to Know About the Inner Lives of Men*. She wrote it based on interviews with over a thousand men, and it challenged me to reconsider some assumptions I had made about my husband and his emotional availability and needs. After reading Chapter 5, "Sex Changes Everything: Why Sex Unlocks a Man's Emotions" (Guess Who Holds the Key?) I had to think about sex differently. I began to think of it as part of the way I keep the lines of communication open with my husband and as something too important to our emotional connection for me to withhold to communicate anger or disappointment. I also started thinking of it as a stress reliever instead of an activity I'm too stressed to engage in. I started to think of it as a crucial item on my to-do list instead of an option that could fall off if life got too busy.

And it wasn't long before our relationship – before I – began to reap the benefits.

Since this will be read by Clarence and a few of his friends, I'll have to preserve some of the details, (a woman has her secrets), but please know the benefits are abundant! Sex with hubby is exactly what Shaunti Feldhahn called it in 2004 – **a key**. And that key has opened doors to new levels between us – in the way we relate to each other, the way we argue, how much more quickly arguments are resolved, how we joke and play with each other, how our feelings are not as easily hurt, how easy it is for me to get him to do what I want (wink wink). Well actually, he is still Clarence, so it can only be so easy to move him in a direction he's not already heading in, but hey, the path to the inner him is certainly a lot clearer these days!

Track 23
Neither One of Us

When you get married in a church, the officiant is likely to declare that you are two becoming one. They may include a metaphor of a rope intertwined to show the strength of unifying two lives and hearts. It's so common that it can be overlooked or discounted, but let's take a moment to unpack this a little.

As you begin to think about what it means for two lives to become one, your first thoughts may go to the fundamental aspects of forming a union like compatibility and love between you and your partner. Because in the beginning we all are full of hope and the desire to do like Keith Sweat sang and make it last forever and ever. As you consider further, more tangible factors that can impact the marriage come to mind like family, culture, or religion. But in truth, there is a laundry list of elements the two will have to reconcile under one roof: health, dating history, personal habits, financial philosophies, spending habits, sexual compatibility (the how and the frequency), personal goals, career/business ambitions, cooking tastes, familial/gender roles, expectations, friends, and so on. Some of these you will (or should) discuss in pre-marital counseling. However, many issues and questions won't be known until you are living together as a unit <u>with the pressure of "forever" weighing on you</u>. The prospect of accommodating another person for a lifetime can be extremely daunting. We all have heard stories of people dating and even living together for years, getting married, and the marriage failing shortly thereafter.

As the days turn into months and months into years, the best intentions for your marriage become strained – <u>multiple times</u>. The things that were just slight irritations become Supreme Court issues in year 5 or 10 or 15. And when reconciling one or more particularly critical issues seems near impossible, you become so disheartened and overwhelmed that during a quiet moment in the car or sitting in the bathroom one morning, you find yourself asking yourself, "Do I really want to be here?"

You may feel a pang of guilt about considering the question. You didn't enter the marriage lightly and you take your commitment seriously. You've spent time and money trying to build something you wanted to be life-long, and now you are wondering if it was all worth it. Much more important than time or money, you've invested **yourself** in this endeavor, and at the moment the investment doesn't seem to be paying off. You might start to reconsider all of the decisions that have brought you to this moment. You think "I don't need this!" or "I could have picked someone else instead of them!" "I'm working so hard to make this work and I don't see them working nearly as hard." "Don't I deserve better?" "Should I leave?"

This uncertainty is not something married people easily talk about. Typically couples only allow the public to see what they want them to see. Marital matters are private and you may be ashamed to have such thoughts. Especially after you have so publicly declared your love for one another. How can there be such trouble in paradise?

When (not if) you find yourself in this position, I want you to please realize the following: All of these thoughts and feelings are 100% normal in every marriage. Every married couple you know, even the ones you admire so much, have similar thoughts and feelings at various times throughout their marriage. Why? Because marriage is a lot of work. Let me repeat that. **MARRIAGE IS A LOT OF WORK.** It weighs on you at times. You rarely hear about the tough sides of marriage, even from your friends. And by the time you do, the relationship is probably in really bad shape.

For me, when things get to the point of questioning staying in the relationship, it weighs on me and my spirit very heavily because I care so deeply; I'm heavily invested. My pride and reputation are at stake. I want this marriage to work. I want it to be great. I want the type of relationship I've dreamed of. It's tempting to use other people's relationships as an indicator of how ours should be. But keep in mind, **people only allow you to see the parts of their relationship that they want you to see.** Our comparison is incomplete at best because we don't have all the details or history of that relationship, no matter how close we think we might be to it. We don't know all that happens behind closed doors. Therefore, we have to remember to run our race. Focus on our race (i.e., relationship) and run it at our pace (i.e., work at it). We base success on what works for us as a couple.

Yalonda and I ran a half-marathon a few years back. We trained for 12 weeks. In the beginning, we trained together, but it became exceedingly difficult because we don't run at the same pace. Eventually, we learned to train at the same time but not at the same pace. Finishing was the goal and, in the end, we both finished the race at a time based on our pace, not in comparison or competition with the other or with any of the other runners.

Equally as important as running our own race is knowing that a good, strong marriage is rarely 50/50 as is commonly said. Rather it's like a pendulum swinging back and forth based on the needs of the individuals involved. Our needs change constantly. Sometimes I need more and sometimes I have more to give. Our pendulum may be at 80/20 one week and 20/80 the next. As long as it's swinging regularly in both directions, we're good. A swinging pendulum means both partners are still actively willing to do the most important thing in a marriage, the work. If it gets stuck on one side for a prolonged period, we may seek counseling (as we have in the past).

So if you've had thoughts about leaving, don't feel bad about them. They are normal. However, don't ignore them. Have a conversation about your feelings. Try to lovingly get to the root of the problem. When people ask us how we've lasted this long, we tell them that in short, the secret sauce is a blend of commitment, continuous and respectful communication, a willingness to see the other person's point of view, and an openness to change. In other words, we have never stopped being willing to do the work.

Track 24
I Wanna Know

In the New Testament, there's a scripture that says, "You have not because you ask not…" Sound advice for a couple. Ask for what you want. Your mate is not a mind reader. My mate does not automatically know my expectations because we love each other. My unspoken expectations are way more likely to go unmet than those I express. How often have I been upset or disappointed with Clarence for not doing what I never asked him to do? I am guilty of thinking, unfairly, "he's known me for this long. How can he not know what I want or what I need?" And then I found myself believing that he was purposely withholding what I wanted from me, or I found myself reading some imagined motive into what he was doing or not doing:

"How dare he not bring me a blanket," I'd think to myself. *He doesn't care* that I'm shivering on this couch." or, "He didn't buy me a nice piece of jewelry this Christmas because *he doesn't think I'm worth it.*"

Assumptions and unspoken expectations like these are landmines for a relationship. If my love language is acts of service or gifts, then I need to express that to him. I can't expect that he should put 2 and 2 together and figure it out based on clues hidden in my words or actions. Especially a person like me who can be pretty stoic, even when I think I'm showing how I feel. I am leaving him to guess what I want, which can seem to him like he's feeling his way through a field of landmines and inevitably he's going to misstep. Boom – disappointment, hurt feelings, arguments, and resentments explode without warning.

So, first, I had to be clear with myself about what I wanted and needed to feel loved and secure. I had to be clear that I want a husband who listens to me talk about a negative experience I've had and acknowledges the feelings I'm expressing **before** bringing up solutions. If my husband has an emotionally charged issue to bring up with me, I need him to be patient while I take time to process it and to be cool with a delayed response. These are needs I had to first recognize within myself before I could articulate them to him. These are things I found myself getting frustrated about, and had to ask myself what would make this situation better for me the next time? The first answer I gave myself was, "It would be better for me if he didn't give me his opinion about anything." Do you know what I mean ladies? But, on second thought, I knew that wasn't what I actually wanted. I do value his opinion, so I want him to share it with me.

I've learned to be specific. I can't just say I want something nice for my birthday or that I want him to bring me home something sweet. I mean I can, and often Clarence is very good at picking jewelry or desserts for me, but I increase my chances of getting what I want to above 97% when I ask for exactly what I want.

I've learned that sometimes I have to ask more than once and extend grace when he doesn't get it right the first time or even the second time. New behaviors take time to become habits. And, new habits are more likely to persist in a kind and loving environment where we have grace for each other's mistakes.

I've learned that I have to check in with myself repeatedly over time. Is what I'm asking for a deal-breaker for me if I don't get it? Can I live with him giving me his version of what I'm asking for? Does what I'm already getting from him outweigh what I'm not getting? Can I do better at demonstrating what I want?

Whether we realize it or not, whether we can verbalize them or not, we each come into the relationship with expectations. Sometimes we can't identify what we expected until we don't get it. We find ourselves upset with our spouse for what they did or didn't do or say, and it takes honest introspection to realize, woah, I never really articulated my expectation or my desire. I assumed that they would "somehow know." Name it and claim it might be overstating it a bit, but certainly, we want to be able to name it and request it if we truly want it.

Track 25

Is it Still Good to Ya?

How many times in your relationship have you had an interaction that went something like this?

Me: Hey, what's wrong?

Her: Nothing.

Me: No, for real, I don't know. What's wrong?

Her: *shrug*

Me: *expressionless emoji*

<Wash, rinse, repeat in various forms>

This type of interaction shows a few things. First, he was observant but clueless. Second, she was upset, disappointed, and at a loss for words. Third and finally, there was a lack of relationship maturity. This type of maturity had nothing to do with our age or how long we'd been together. It was merely an area of our relationship where we had yet to grow. If you were watching 2 kids having this interaction, you would probably find yourself laughing. And that's my point. We had to grow.

There are times when you are bothered by something your spouse has done. They keep cutting you off in conversation or leaving the toilet seat up or devaluing your opinion or leaving the bed unmade. To you, their actions are blatant and obvious. You think, how could they do this, and even worse, how could they act oblivious and think what they did wouldn't upset you? You wonder if they are purposely being obtuse. Now you're not only upset by the offense, you're doubly offended by their nerve to behave in a dim-witted way afterward.

News Flash: These are the types of thoughts that can keep areas of your relationship from maturing. How can your spouse know what's bothering you if you don't articulate it? If they are asking, give them the benefit of the doubt that they want to hear what you have to say. And on the other hand, don't ask if you don't genuinely want to know in order to attempt to rectify it.

Everyone is not affected the same by the same situation. Everyone has a unique background and a unique set of experiences that cause them to process information through their own lens. They come to their own conclusions. They legitimately may not know they did anything wrong. They may recognize what they did, but not think it has or should have upset you. They may have a blind spot in that area. You don't know, because you only know how you've felt about what has happened and that you're upset.

This is one of the simplest lessons of marriage I can give you. If they ask what's wrong, tell them. If you're not ready to talk, ask for more time. Find your words and tell them. Give your partner a chance to respond. Trust that they can receive your answer in love. It may lead to a deeper discussion. It may confirm everything you thought to be true. OR It may lead to an apology or an explanation. Regardless, **IT WILL** lead to better insight into one another for the next time that situation arises.

Bonus Track
Get Wisdom

Yalonda and I eloped when we got married. Although everyone knew we were engaged, the anxiety of the wedding planning with one of us a student living 300 miles away was putting so much strain on us that we decided to forgo it and made an appointment to be married by the Justice of the Peace. We didn't tell anyone. Two days before our courthouse appointment, we went to dinner with her father, who was also a church elder. He was often out preaching so Yalonda and I met him at a spot near the church, a restaurant we had never been to before but was easy to find.

It wasn't an upscale dinner because her dad was a pretty simple guy. The dinner was at a little cafeteria-style diner in the hood of Baltimore City. The kind of place where you pay for the food by the pound. I remember his meal – whiting, mac & cheese, green beans, two dinner rolls, and a half & half. We'd spent time with her dad and family before, but this was a new experience for me because it was going to be just the three of us and not their whole family. It turned out to be pretty cool and fun. Her dad was a gregarious and jovial guy so dinner conversation flowed with ease.

Halfway through dinner, things took a slight turn. What we thought was going to be a "get to know each other better" dinner turned unknowingly into our one and only pre-marital couples counseling session right in the middle of the crowded dining room. He began to give us his thoughts on marriage from both a biblical and practical perspective. Honestly, it's been so long ago that I don't remember all that was said. However, one of his statements was so simple yet so profound that it has become a cornerstone for our marriage. It's the one piece of advice I give to couples considering marriage. He said,

"There are only two things that break up a marriage. Sex and Money – Too much of one or not enough of the other."

I was blown away by how such a simple statement could have such broad application. While I'm sure some will disagree, I have found this statement to be true in every divorce I've known the details of in some form or fashion. Extramarital sex. Too much time spent working making plenty of money, but therefore, not enough sex. Not enough money because one was spending or gambling it all. Not enough sex because you couldn't agree on how to manage the money. And on and on. I'm sure you can think of a few other ways this statement has played out.

My father-in-law's simple statement taught us to confront sex and money issues as quickly as we can whenever they arise. Because I think it was his way of telling us that sex and money problems are often manifestations of a fundamental lack of balance in a relationship. So far, it's helped us last more than 25 years. Wise words from a wise man.

Rest in Power K.B.

Outro

We hope you enjoyed and gleaned a little something from us sharing our lessons learned with you. We don't think any single lesson is more important than any other. All of them have their place in our life/marriage.

Whether you're married or not, everyone knows that maintaining long-term relationships comes with inherent challenges. While you may consider your challenges unique, the likelihood is they are not. We all share multiple threads of commonality with each other and, consequently, we can learn from each other. Do you need to make a specific mistake in order to learn from it or can you learn from someone else's mistake? Similarly, what is working for another couple may also work for you.

We challenge you to read this book (or even select Tracks) with other strong couples you know. Let it be a conversation starter about the various topics presented. The key themes we wanted to highlight were communication, openness, introspection, forgiveness, vulnerability, friendship, humor, and of course love (as a word that has action behind it, not just a feeling).

We also challenge you to put together a list of things you've learned in your relationship. It's an exercise we'd suggest because it turned out to be fun quality time for us and, like us, you may come away from it with new insights about yourselves and your relationship. We'd hope those insights would lead to a greater appreciation of each other's differences, clearer recognition of the compromise and sacrifices you've each made or need to make for the sake of the relationship, an acknowledgment of what you've enjoyed and endured together, and finally, a commitment to do the work to keep your relationship going the full distance. In short, we hope you come away from reading this book, and from engaging in a similar exercise as we did in writing it, with a stronger bond.

Our approach to problem-solving is pretty simple. Look out for the needs of the other person as much as possible. If I'm truly looking out for you and you are truly looking out for me, there is no need for either of us to selfishly look out for ourselves. It's much easier said than done and we have been working on it for 25 years... and counting.

Lastly, if you haven't figured it out, each of the track titles is an actual song title. We created a Spotify playlist of these songs for you to enjoy. We also included songs contributed by the amazing HeartBEATS family. To listen, use the QR Code below or go to: https://sptfy.com/TheRhythmOfLove

Connect with the Authors

Website: www.cylentertainment.com

Facebook: www.facebook.com/CYLEntertainment

Instagram: www.instagram.com/cylentertainment

Twitter: www.twitter.com/CYLEntertainme2

Linktr.ee: www.linktr.ee/contactcylent

Creative Control With Self-Publishing

Divine Legacy Publishing provides authors with the guid-ance necessary to take creative control of their work through self-publishing. We provide:

Writing Coaching

Professional Editing

Author Branding

Self-Publishing Coaching

Graphic Design

Website Design

Let Divine Legacy Publishing help you master the business of self-publishing.